IMAGES OF ENGLAND

Around Alfreton

ALFRETON PARISH

NOTT^M	ALFR^N
16	0
MILES	MILES

The famous turnpike road sign located outside the George Hotel in the old market place, Alfreton. Dating from c.1785, the post was located here as The George was the meeting place for the Turnpike Trustees.

IMAGES OF ENGLAND

Around Alfreton

Alfreton and District Heritage Trust

NONSUCH

This dragon is on the roof of the old Town Hall on High Street. Although the picture is a recent one, the dragon dates back to c.1896, when this famous building was constructed.

First published 1994
This new pocket edition 2006
Images unchanged from first edition

Nonsuch Publishing Limited
The Mill, Brimscombe Port,
Stroud, Gloucestershire, GL5 2QG
www.nonsuch-publishing.com

Nonsuch Publishing is an imprint of Tempus Publishing Group

British Library Cataloguing in Publication Data.
A catalogue record for this book is available from the British Library.

ISBN 1-84588-244-X

Typesetting and origination by Nonsuch Publishing Limited

Contents

Wray's Tailors shop at the junction of High Street and Bonsall Lane. This later became Verney's Tailors Shop. In more recent times the building has been used by Stanley H. Fields as an opticians, later as an employment agency, and currently as an estate agent.

Introduction

The idea of establishing a Heritage Centre in Alfreton was first discussed amongst the members of the Rotary Club Of Alfreton during the winter of 1983. Following an exploratory meeting with a member of another Heritage Centre and examining correspondence with the Civic Trust and other publications, it was decided to hold a public meeting to ascertain local feelings about such a project.

On 10 February 1984, a meeting was held at Cressy Fields attended by over forty people including the County Archivist and the County Curator. The idea received an enthusiastic response and a steering committee was formed. An application was then made to the Charity Commissioners and the Alfreton and District Heritage Trust was officially registered as a charity.

In 1984 it was hoped that it might be possible to develop a Heritage Centre in Alfreton House, one of the oldest buildings in Alfreton, dating back to c.1649. This and several successive schemes proved abortive. However, in 1990 a booklet was produced by the Trust called *History around Alfreton*. This proved to be a great success and gave a fresh impetus to the idea of a Heritage Centre. Subsequently, in 1993, the Trust was offered the use of the Cemetery Chapel, Rodgers Lane, Alfreton as a Heritage Centre and on 3 July 1993, the Alfreton and District Heritage Centre was officially opened by Councillor Charles Cutting, Mayor of Amber Valley Borough Council. The day was a great success and the Heritage Centre has since opened every Sunday between 2.00pm and 4.00pm.

In 1994 the Trust produced a set of eight postcards called 'Old Alfreton'. The cards dated from 1895 to 1957, and reproduced some of the most popular pictures on display at the Heritage Centre. Shortly after this we were approached by David Buxton of Tempus Publishing Group to put together this book based on a collection of old photographs of the Alfreton area.

We hope the finished book gives you a good insight into days gone by.

Richard Roughton
Chairman, Alfreton and District Heritage Trust

Acknowledgements

Compiling this collection of photographs would not have been possible without the generous support of the people in and around the district of Alfreton. Special thanks go the the following:

Hugh Mackenzie, the original Chairman of the Steering Committee from 1983 until 1993 when he was elected President of the Trust. Without his dedication and determination, the Trust would not have been kept alive.

Adrian Knifton and Don Watson for their time and effort in collating the collection of photographs and providing the original captions.

Mr F. Alvey and Mr E. Williamson for providing inspiration at their slide shows of Old Alfreton.

Fellow members of the Alfreton and District Heritage Trust.

Members of the public for their kind donations and loans of photographs and artefacts on display at the Alfreton Heritage Centre.

Alfreton and District Heritage Centre, The Heritage Chapel, Rodgers Lane, Alfreton, is open every Sunday from 2.00pm to 4.00pm, and at other times by arrangement. If you have any artefacts to donate or loan, have any information to contribute, or would like to become a member, please visit us. Admission is free.

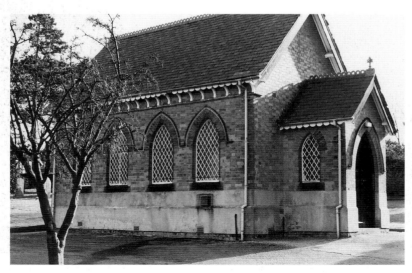

Cemetery Chapel, now Alfreton and District Heritage Centre.

One

The Old Market Place and Church Street

The top of King Street in the early 1900s, showing the Old Moot Hall on the left. The road was only twelve feet wide between the buildings, making access difficult.

The Moot Hall in 1910. The earliest reference to this building is 1646. It was used as a court house and later converted to a market hall, being demolished in 1914.

The top of King Street in the early 1900s, showing Moot Hall on the right and W. Lowe's saddle shop on the left.

The Market Place in the early 1900s; Redfern's shop can be seen next to Moot Hall. The building on the left is now the National Westminster Bank, which was built in 1892.

This photograph was taken about 1915 after Moot Hall had been demolished.

The junction with Church Street in the early 1900s.

This photograph was taken from Chesterfield Road prior to 1914.

Looking towards Church Street during one of the Horse Fairs in 1905.

Church Street, c. 1910; on the left is the Congregational Church leading to Alfreton Hall and the Parish Church.

Left: Market day. The last market on this site was held in 1954.

Below: The new market site on Institute Lane in 1974.

Above: The unveiling of the war memorial on 31 July 1927 by General Sir Horace Smith-Dorien. Over 20,000 people attended the event.

Right: The war memorial after the unveiling.

Above: These cottages were on Church Street in about 1960 and have since been demolished.

Left: The back of an old cottage showing the one and only door to the building.

Looking down Church Street towards the Old Market Place in 1913.

Alfreton, Park Gate.

The Lodge, Church Street, in 1914. The road on the right leads to the Parish Church while the road on the left is the main entrance to Alfreton Hall.

The first Vicarage on Church Street was built over 500 years ago and is now privately owned.

THE VICARAGE, ALFRETON.

This is the second vicarage, built in 1891. It later became the Glebe Aged Persons' home when the present Vicarage was built in 1951.

Two

King Street
and Chesterfield Road

At the top of King Street, *c.* 1910, showing Brewers Croft on the right at the back of the bill-boards, between the Royal Oak and the Four Horse Shoes. The second shop on the left was the saddlers.

The Horse Fair on King Street in 1902.

A parade outside the Four Horse Shoes, around 1900, showing the Church Lads' Brigade.

On the left of the picture, taken in 1890, the bank is being built. It later became the National Westminster Bank.

A view down King Street, 1890.

Left: Fell's rope shop at the junction of Hall Street and King Street.

Below: A horse fair in the early 1900s. Part of the King's Head Inn sign can be seen on the left.

This was Thomas Painter's farm, shop, and public house in the 1890s. The public house was demolished in 1899 and the Railway Hotel was built on the site in 1901.

Thomas Painter's original cottage, which is still standing.

Alfreton Fire Brigade outside their King Street station with Joby Spencer in the centre. The building later became the Council Offices and is now a factory.

Colliery Road from Derby Road showing the Old Police Station on the right. This was demolished and the Abraham Lincoln Library was built on the site in 1940 as part of the Robert Watchorn Estate.

The Devonshire in 1920. Devonshire Terrace can be seen at the rear, and was demolished to make way for new housing.

The Old House of Confinement in 1905, which was used as a prison. In the background is Webster's Row. The old thatched cottage on the left was replaced by Coronation Cottages, which are dated 22 June 1911.

Cottages below the House of Confinement in the early 1900s.

A horse and carriage outside the house of Mr W.J. Whysall.

Wingfield Road in 1910. The families in the cottage were the Brooks and the Attenboroughs.

Wingfield Road, c.1924.

A row of cottages near Independent Hill in the early 1900s.

THE DERBY ROAD, ALFRETON.

At the junction of the road to Oakerthorpe in the early 1900s.

Robert Watchorn, a local lad who emigrated to America and made his fortune. He never forgot the place where he was born and remains Alfreton's best-known benefactor. He was born on 5 April 1858 in the second cottage of Bacon's Yard, Alfreton. His family were poor and he worked at Shirland Colliery until the age of twenty-two when he set sail for America. Settling in Pennsylvania, he worked in the mines and became secretary of the local trade union. By the turn of the century, he had become a wealthy public figure. He married Alma Jessica in Columbus, Ohio, on 30 June 1891. Sadly his first son, Robert Kinnear Watchorn, died in infancy. His second son, Ewart Watchorn, died on 10 July 1921. Robert Watchorn often returned home to Alfreton and built memorials to his family in the form of a church, a park, a library and playing fields. Several streets in Alfreton are also named after his family including Alma Street and Ewart's Lane. Robert Watchorn died in California on 13 April 1944.

Left: The cottage where Robert Watchorn was born, 2 Bacons Yard, Derby Road.

Below: The playing fields which were dedicated to the memory of his son Emory Ewart.

MEMORIAL PARK, ALFRETON.   G.2528.

Bacons Yard. This was later demolished to be replaced by the Watchorn Church in 1929.

Part of the playing fields which disappeared in 1969 to make way for the A38 Alfreton bypass.

The Watchorn primitive Methodist Church, built in 1929. On the opposite side of the road is the Alma Watchorn Memorial Park in memory of Robert's wife.

The Abraham Lincoln Library, built in memory of the American President in 1940. During the war it was used as a hospital, and sadly it has never since been used as a library.

The Church of England School on Chesterfield Road taken during the 1980s, long after its use as a school was discontinued. Built in 1846 and extended during 1874, it was demolished in the 1980s to make way for new housing.

Inside the Church of England School during 1927, when the headmaster was Mr Thompson.

The staff of the Church of England School with the headmaster, Mr Helliwell.

The toll bar house on Chesterfield Road at the junction of Westhouses Lane. After a final collision with a heavy goods vehicle it was demolished during the 1960s.

Three

Alfreton Hall

Alfreton Hall was built for George Morewood in 1724 by Francis Smith of Warwick and was extended in 1796. In 1854 the east wing was added. The Palmer-Morewood family lived at the Hall until 1957, when it was sold to Derbyshire County Council for £28,500. The original west wing, containing the ballroom and twenty-five rooms, was demolished in 1968 due to mining subsidence. Only the east wing extension exists today which is used as an adult education centre.

Above: The entrance to Alfreton Hall on Church Street in 1919.

Left: A portrait of Helen Morewood, the widow of George Morewood. She later remarried to the Reverend Henry Case, Rector of Ladbroke in County Warwick, and died in 1824. She was succeeded by her nephew William Palmer who assumed the name of Morewood and became the first Palmer-Morewood.

ALFRETON PARK.

Above: The complete Hall showing the east wing extension on the right.

Right: The Reverend Henry Case, who married Helen Morewood.

Above: The interior of the Hall.

Left: Charles Rowland Palmer-Morewood, who was born in 1843 and succeeded his father as squire of Alfreton in 1873. He married Patience Mary, the third daughter of Lord Hervey of Bristol in 1873. They had a son, Rowland Charles (born in 1879), and a daughter, Clara (born in 1881). He died in Paris in 1910.

Above: The interior of Alfreton Hall when it was in its prime.

Right: The Hon. Patience Hervey, daughter of Lord Hervey of Bristol, who married Charles Rowland Palmer-Morewood in 1873.

Above: Alfreton Hall and gardens during the early 1900s.

Left: Rowland Charles Palmer Morewood at the age of fourteen in 1893. He married the daughter of Reverend De Cas, vicar of Alfreton. He died in 1957, which led to the sale of the Hall.

Alfreton Hall from Lake.

Above: Alfreton Hall lake in 1903. This was converted into a swimming pool in 1934 and later modified into the current Alfreton Lido in 1964.

Right: Clara Palmer-Morewood at the age of twelve in 1893.

Horses and carriage outside the Hall around the turn of the twentieth century.

Rowland Charles Palmer-Morewood with visitors in 1939.

Above: Alfreton Hall Gardens.

Right: A roadway through Alfreton Park leading from the Church Street lodge to the Wingfield Road lodge. It is now the entrance to the Leisure Centre.

The demolition of the west wing due to subsidence in 1968.

Alfreton Hall Adult Education Centre in 1969.

44

Four

High Street

Taken from a painting of around 1850, High Street with Alfreton House on the right.

A group of local people outside Alfreton House, c.1890.

Alfreton House, built between 1649 and 1660, was originally the Gate Inn and later became a private residence.

Right: Firs House, once the home of Alderman Mortimer Wilson who entered the legal profession and became a county councillor. His work as chairman of the county education committee led to the local comprehensive school being named after him.

Below: A garden party at the Firs in 1904.

Above: The Radford family outside their farm house on High Street at the junction with Cressy Road.

Left: Next to the old Town Hall, this house is now the Halifax Building Society.

Looking towards Nottingham Road with Alfreton House on the left.

The old post office and town hall at the junction of High Street and Cressy Road in 1912.

At the junction with Rodgers Lane showing Radford's farm and Alfreton House in 1957. The farm was built in the 1680s and demolished in 1964 to make way for a block of shops.

Radford's Farm in the early 1960s.

Above: Rodgers Lane in 1957 looking towards Cressy Road.

Right: Cemetery Lane, now Rodgers Lane, in the winter of 1935-6.

Cressy Road, c.1905.

Cressy Road, c.1905; obviously very popular at the time.

At the junction of Cressy Road in the early 1900s. There are no shops on the right hand side; most of the shops were built in the 1920s.

High Street, Alfreton, in the 1930s showing The Traveller's Rest on the left. This was demolished in 1935 to make way for the King Alfred Hotel, built on the same site. It has been known as Ye Olde McDonald's Farm since 1993.

The Empire Cinema, photographed here about 1930, was opened in 1922 and demolished in 1986 to make way for new shops.

From the junction with Limes Avenue, c.1915. A steam wagon can be seen on the road. Shops on the left include Challoner's butchers, Loverocks, The Piper Penny Bazaar, and Hunter's Tea Stores.

The Traveller's Rest Inn at the junction with Chapel Street. The licensee was Mr A. Morton. Was the man in the right-hand doorway very tall, or was it a very small door?

Near Institute Lane in 1914. Now the site of Boots the Chemist and the Electricity Board.

High Street in the 1940s, with the King Alfred on the right and the Empire Cinema on the left.

Near the top of Institute Lane in 1961.

The opening of the memorial fountain by Melvyn Watson, erected in memory of Dr John Joseph Bingham. Originally located at the corner of Limes Avenue, it was later moved to its present site on the Welfare ground in 1937 when Burton's Tailors and Woolworths were built.

Welfare and Schools, Alfreton.

The present site of the memorial fountain to Dr Bingham.

Next to the King Alfred Hotel in 1961. The houses in the background were in Chapel Street and have since been demolished.

Institute Lane in the 1950s.

The public toilets in Institute Lane, c.1969. Now the site of Boots the Chemist.

Mill Close School on Institute Lane in 1969. The school was built in 1890 and closed in 1973.

Above: Sunday School procession in 1895 near Institute Lane. The car belonged to Dr Corkery and was one of the first in Alfreton. His surgery and house were next to the Blue Bell Inn and were demolished to make way for the Royal Cinema.

Left: The corner of New Street in the early 1900s.

SAML. ABBOTT & SON, High St., ALFRETON.
Auctioneers, Accountants, Rent and Debt Collectors, Certificated Bailiffs, House and Land Agents, Bill Posting Contractors (Four Miles' Circuit).

A procession in High Street, *c.*1900.

A procession in the early 1900s on the day of a cattle market. Dr Bingham's house was on the left, where Woolworths stands today.

Looking towards Church Street, *c.*1907. No queues of traffic meant people could walk around freely!

Dr Bingham's car outside his house in the 1920s.

This was the era of the horse and cart showing the Wesleyan chapel, now the site of the Yorkshire Bank.

Near the junction of King Street in 1925. In the 1970s, these stood derelict and boarded up, eventually being demolished to make way for the new Post Office in the early 1980s.

From the old Market Place in 1892. The scaffolding on the left was for the new bank, then under construction.

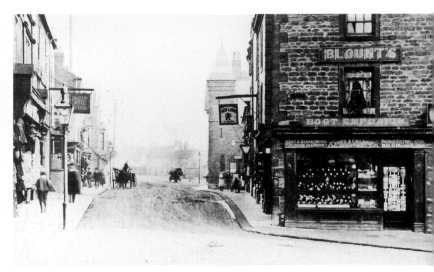

The junction of King Street and High Street in 1900.

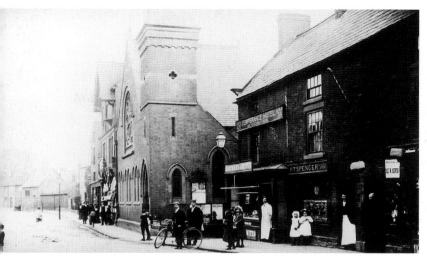

The Wesleyan church in 1910. This was demolished in the 1980s to make way for the Yorkshire Bank.

The Castle Hotel on the left, where W. Fletcher was in residence between 1912 and 1920.

The Royal Cinema, built in 1930 on the site of Dr Corkery's house, at the corner of Institute Lane next to the Bluebell Inn. It was opened on 16 April 1931 by Mr R.A. Palmer-Morewood. In 1936 it was renamed the Odeon.

The Odeon had 1,750 seats including a large circle. It closed on 30 May 1964 and was demolished in 1965 to be replaced by modern shops.

Five

Shops and Industry

General Grocers, *c.*1915. This is now Currys.

Above: Challoner's butchers at the corner of Limes Avenue. This is now Barclays Bank.

Left: Buxton's fishmongers and fruiterer near to the junction of Bonsall Lane. This is now the Trustee Savings Bank.

LOVEROCK & SON,

General Drapers,
Milliners,
Clothiers,
and Outfitters.

Telephone **50.**

ALFRETON.

Advert for Loverock and Son, general drapers, on High Street in 1925.

The Globe Tea Co. in the early 1900s, situated between George Street and Cressy Road.

Left: Professor Peat's music shop, *c.*1915, next to the Castle Hotel.

Below: An advert for G. Hemsley, family grocer on High Street.

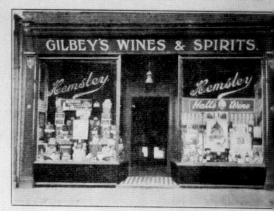

G. HEMSLEY,
FAMILY GROCER

HIGH-CLASS
Groceries
and Provisions

At Lowest Market Prices.

AGENT for
W. & A. GILBEY.

Telephone 22.

HIGH STREET, ALFRETON.

Above: Wood's Sweet Shop, which closed in the 1960s. The Electricity Board showroom is now on this site.

Right: E. Woodhead and Sons, general grocers. A familiar site in those days was the bacon and hams hung outside the shop.

Above: The Market Café and Currys in 1955. A previous owner of the Café, Mr Brown, is pictured on the left with Mr Thorpe, a bookmaker.

Left: Eastmans Ltd. and Extons. The building was next to the site of the current Yorkshire Bank.

Above: Part of the dining room in the Market Café in 1955.

Right: W.M. Marsh, ladies' and gentlemen's tailors.

Dyson's Chemists in the 1930s.

A row of shops in 1930, on the site of the new Post Office. Will Spencer is standing in the doorway of the Tobacconist and Hairdresser's shop which he owned.

Above: Verney's shop at the junction of Bonsall Lane in the early 1900s.

Right: Near to the junction with Bonsall Lane, the London City and Midland Bank Ltd amalgamated with the Nottingham Joint Stock Bank in 1906. It is now the site of the Derbyshire Building Society.

Winn's Bakery in the old Market Place in the early 1900s. In 1895 it had been Breffit's Bakery and later in the 1930s it became Wildes Bakery.

Charles Jones, family grocer, lower King Street. The shop opened in 1890 as a bakery selling bread in his own shops located in Wilson Street and Prospect Street. The business continued in the hands of his son. This shop was demolished in the 1960s and replaced by housing.

Right: In the old Market Place, now the site of the Midland Bank.

Below: A. Smith's shop in King Street which sold china and general goods.

Left: Burnham's — plumber, decorator and gas fitter, in King Street.

Below: Lower King Street in 1928, Limb's Paper Shop is on the right. It was on the site now occupied by Haddon Close.

Above: Nelson Dawes and Les Marriot standing outside Dawes Butcher's Shop on Nottingham Road in 1925.

Right: Hunter's Tea Stores and grocers in Church Street. It is now a fitness centre.

Alfreton Colliery in 1920. It was opened in 1886 as one of the Blackwell Colliery Company mines. When it closed on September 28th 1968, it employed 652 men. It was situated at the bottom of Meadow Lane and is now an industrial estate.

Cotes Park Colliery, opened in 1850 and closed in 1963. It is now the site of the Cotes Park Industrial Estate.

Six

Churches

The Parish Church of St. Martin was built about 1170, and is the oldest building in Alfreton. Major additions were made in 1868 and it is still very much a part of the town's heritage.

The interior of St. Martin's church before the major alterations made in 1868. It shows the chancel with the organ on the left. The arch and the stained glass east window were moved back to enlarge the church.

The church choir in 1921, with the Reverend Louis De Cas and the Bishop of Southwell.

Taken in 1927, the railings were removed during the war in the 1940s.

The interior of St. Chad's Mission Church in Mansfield Road, taken in 1916. It was known locally as the 'Tin Tabernacle'.

The foundation stone for the new Church Hall being laid on 16 July 1913 by James Oakes Esq., J.P. The Hall was demolished in June 1994. St Chad's church can be seen in the background, which has also now been demolished.

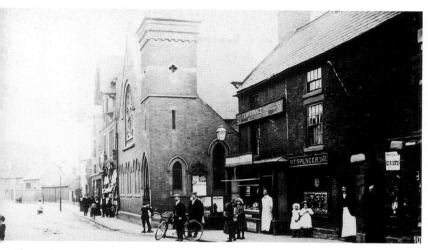

The Wesleyan Church in 1910. The church was built in 1885 and demolished in 1983 to make way for the Yorkshire Bank. The main leaded light windows and other parts were saved and incorporated into the new Wesleyan Church built at the junction of Nottingham Road and Ellesmere Avenue.

Outside the Wesleyan Church in 1908.

The Primitive Methodist Chapel and Manse in Derby road. It was built in 1853 and demolished in 1928 to make way for the Watchorn Methodist Church, which was built in 1929 on the same site.

The Derby Road Primitive Methodist Chapel choir in 1920.

Right: The Congregational Church pictured in 1959. In the 1960s the top of the tower was removed for safety reasons. The church is now known as the United Reformed Church.

Below: Inside the Congregational Church.

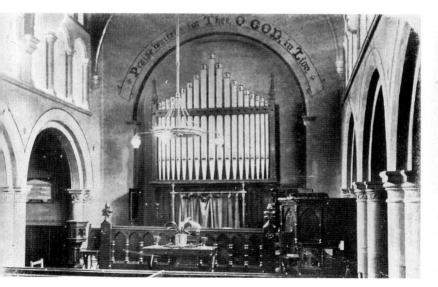

The Ebenezer Methodist Church at the junction of Nottingham Road and Orange Street taken in the early 1900s. Built in 1881, it closed in 1970 and is now the home of Thornton's Printers.

One of the few surviving interior pictures of the Ebenezer Methodist Church.

The Watchorn Primitive Methodist Church in Derby Road, built in 1929 as part of the Robert Watchorn Memorial Estate.

Inside the Watchorn Church.

The choir of the Roman Catholic Church in procession along Nottingham Road in the early 1900s.

The opening of the new Assemblies of God Church in Hall Street with Pastor Colliss.

Seven

Mansfield Road and Nottingham Road

The junction of Nottingham Road and Mansfield Road in 1912. The whole row of houses has now been demolished, albeit in two stages. Aged persons' flats have now been built on the site.

A decorated dray in Ted Smith's coal yard in 1923, at the top of Wycliffe Road near to the junction with Nottingham Road. The picture was taken during one of the regular Whitsuntide Sunday School processions.

The Gate Inn, Nottingham Road. The cottages on the left next to the shop have since been demolished.

At the junction of Prospect Street and Nottingham Road in 1910. The New Roman Catholic Church now stands on the left.

Thompson's removal cart near Prospect Street, c.1900.

A procession in 1900 at the junction of Prospect Street.

NOTTINGHAM ROAD ALFRETON.

The Gables, built in 1898. This photograph was taken in 1910.

At the junction with Flowery Leys Lane in 1910.

Key's Farm on Nix's Hill which is now part of the Industrial Estate.

Manfield Road in 1910; then it was safe for children to play in the road.

Mansfield Road in the early 1900s. On the left were the printing works belonging to the Sharpe family, who also owned a commercial college in Ellesmere Avenue. The cottages are still standing today.

A Sunday School procession on Prospect Street. The Station Hotel (now the Golden Arrow) can be seen on the left.

The Mid-Derbyshire Manufacturing Co. on Manfield Road. Left to right: Mr Pashley, George Jackson, Joe Johnson (known as 'Tinker'), Albert Bancroft, Joe Morton and Frank Spaven.

An ice cream cart on Abbott Road.

Eight

Transport

Alfreton Midland Railway Station in 1920. The line first opened in 1865 and the station was built in the 1890s.

The opening of Alfreton Railway Station in the 1890s.

The station in 1920. It was a victim of the Beeching Axe in the 1960s and was eventually demolished. In 1972 it was rebuilt and opened as Alfreton and Mansfield Parkway. In 1994 new signs appeared, simply referring to it as Alfreton Station. It had been decided to reopen the Robin Hood Line and so Mansfield will get its own station.

The staff of the station in the early 1900s.

The fifteen staff of Alfreton Station at the turn of the twentieth century.

A Jubilee Class 45562 'Albert' express passenger train at Alfreton Station in 1966.

Tom Marshall's horse and cart.

Alfreton Urban District Council's lorry in 1930 with the surveyor, Mr Ward.

A council water lorry.

Parish Church. Alfreton

The car belonging to Mr Palmer-Morewood of Alfreton Hall outside the Parish Church.

Tom Marshall from the Waggon and Horse's Hotel advertising his private car for hire in Marshall Street.

Tom Marshall with his private hire car.

The first bus belonging to Alfreton Motor Transport in 1910.

This photograph was taken in 1923. The Trent Motor Traction Co. was formed in 1913 and began a service from Alfreton to Derby.

Naylor's bus service to Mansfield in the early 1920s. The bus stands near to the junction of Institute Lane and High Street. This picture is well known to many people of Alfreton.

Alfreton Transport buses in the old Market Place during the 1930s.

A Trent bus in Institute Lane in 1956.

Taken in the 1960s, the old bus station in Institute Lane at the back of the Odeon Cinema.

The Institute Lane Bus Station in 1971. This was later to be demolished when Hillards Superstore and the new Market Hall were built.

Transport on King Street, 1920.

Workmen with their steam roller in Mansfield Road.

Nine

Local Villages
around Alfreton

Beastall's off licence at Somercotes Corner in 1905.

Pennytown, Somercotes, so named because the residents paid one silver penny as rent. Pennytown was demolished in the early 1970s to be replaced by an industrial estate.

COTES PARK

A walk alongside the Shady ponds at Cotes Park, Somercotes. The area has recently been re-established into a nature reserve and is now known as Pennytown ponds.

The Three Horse Shoes public house at Leabrook's Corner. Not too different to how it appears today.

Coupland Place, Somercotes, in the early 1960s. It has since been demolished and a new housing estate built on the site.

The old toll bar house near to Sleetmore Lane on Derby Road between Swanwick and Alfreton. It was severely damaged by a lorry and consequently demolished.

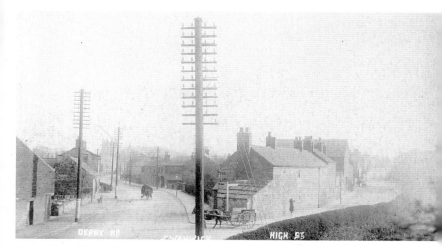

The junction of Derby Road and High Street, Swanwick, in the early 1900s.

Swanwick Hayes was built in 1850 by Francis Wright. It became a conference centre about 1910 and, for a short period during the First World War, was used as barracks. During the Second World War the Hayes accommodated British troops before being converted into a prison camp. It was from here that the only German prisoner of war to escape from an English camp managed to get away. Since the war it has developed into a world-famous conference centre.

Swanwick Hall, c.1914. The Hall was built in the sixteenth century and was once the home of the Turner family. It has been used as a school since 1922.

Riddings Mills, c. 1910. The Mills were built by James Oakes in 1877 and were named James and Sarah after Mr Oakes and his wife. They stood in front of the Diversey factory on Greenhill Lane and were demolished following a fire in 1963.

Codnor Park Monument, *c.*1900, erected around 1844 in memory of William Jessop, an engineer and the manager of The Butterley Company. It is still standing today but is on private land and cannot be accessed by the public partially due to its unsafe condition.

Carnfield Hall in 1907. This building, which dates from the fifteenth century and was later rebuilt in the Elizabethan style, was the home of the Revell family for over 200 years. During the twentieth century it has changed hands several times: an engineering firm bought it for use as a training centre, and the last owner, James Cartland (a relative of Barbara Cartland), carried out substantial renovation before opening it to the public for a short time.

The Revell family.

The garden of Carnfield Hall, c.1908.

The village of South Normanton in 1916.

Crich Stand, c.1900. The original tower was built by Frances Hurt of Alderwasley in 1788, and in 1851 it was rebuilt further back from the cliff edge. Shortly after this picture was taken in 1902 it was struck by lightning.

Crich Stand, the present tower, which was erected in 1923 as a war memorial to members of the
Nottinghamshire and Derbyshire Sherwood Foresters Regiment who lost their lives in the Great War.

The ruins of Wingfield Manor, *c.*1908. The Manor was built by Ralph, Lord Cromwell, in the fifteenth century. Mary Queen of Scots was imprisoned here in 1569, and again in 1584-5.At the time of writing the house is undergoing renovation.

The famous crypt of Wingfield Manor, *c.*1900.

Ten

Farms

Hunts Farm off Flowery Leys Lane in the 1940s. It has since been demolished.

An old farmyard at the top of Mansfield Road. it was replaced by a car showroom and garage which was formerly owned by Greasleys and Kettles, and is now owned by Draycotts.

Cotes Park Farm showing the Colliery tip. After the pit was closed in 1963, the area became an industrial estate.

Griffin Radford's Farm at the corner of High Street and Rodgers Lane in the 1940s. It was built in the 1680s and was pulled down to make way for a shopping complex.

An outbuilding at Radford's Farm.

Griffin Radford and his wife with land girls during the Second World War.

Mr Radford with land-girl Freda Snape in the 1940s.

The stables at Hall Farm, Church Street.

The entrance to Hall Farm, next to the Parish church.